play guitar w[ith]
the cor[rs]

Wise Publications
London/New York/Paris/Sydney/Copenhagen/Madrid/Tokyo

Music Sales Limited
8-9 Frith Street,
London W1V 5TZ, England.
Music Sales Pty Limited
120 Rothschild Avenue,
Rosebery, NSW 2018, Australia.

Order No. AM960971
ISBN 0-7119-7865-4
This book © Copyright 1999
by Wise Publications

Music compiled and arranged by Arthur Dick
Music processed by Andrew Shiels
Cover photographs courtesy of
All Action and Rex Features

Printed in the United Kingdom by
Caligraving Limited, Thetford, Norfolk.

CD programmed by John Moores
Recorded by Kester Sims
Guitar preparation by Charlie Chandler at Chandler Guitars
All guitars by Arthur Dick
Violin by Dermot Crehan
With special thanks to Andy Milner at *Marshall* for supply of amplification

Your Guarantee of Quality
As publishers, we strive to produce
every book to the highest commercial standards.
The music has been freshly engraved and the book has
been carefully designed to minimise awkward page turns
and to make playing from it a real pleasure.
Particular care has been given to specifying acid-free,
neutral-sized paper made from pulps which have not been
elemental chlorine bleached. This pulp is from farmed
sustainable forests and was produced with
special regard for the environment.
Throughout, the printing and binding have been planned
to ensure a sturdy, attractive publication which
should give years of enjoyment.
If your copy fails to meet our high standards,
please inform us and we will gladly replace it.

www.playguitarwith.com
www.musicsales.co.uk

Music Sales' complete catalogue describes thousands of titles
and is available in full colour sections by subject, direct from
Music Sales Limited. Please state your areas of interest
and send a cheque/postal order for £1.50 for postage to:
Music Sales Limited, Newmarket Road,
Bury St. Edmunds, Suffolk IP33 3YB.

guitars, effects and set-up

Arthur Dick describes his recording techniques for the accompanying CD

erin shore (intro)

The lead part (in unison with the violin and whistle) was played on a
Taylor 514-C fitted with a Fishman 'Blender' pickup/mic system.

forgiven, not forgotten

Both rhythm and lead parts were played on a Tom Anderson Custom Shop guitar.
The rhythm used a clean sound from a MesaBoogie TriAxis with lots of
TC Electronic spatial chorusing. A *Line 6* POD provided the heavier lead sound.
The settings were as follows:
Amp model: Rectified. Drive:3. Bass:1. Mid:3. Treble:8. Reverb:off (add at mix).
Effect - compressor:5.
Additional overdubs came from a Les Paul Custom and '62 Strat into the TriAxis.

only when i sleep

Two acoustic tracks using the Taylor (varying the blend of mic and pickup) were
recorded first. An additional rhythm track using a Gibson ES335 into the TriAxis
(rhythm yellow mode) was then added to fill out the basic track.
The lead parts were played on the Les Paul (rhythm pickup), firstly into the
TriAxis with a fair amount of gain (Lead 2 green mode) then the POD
with the following settings:
Amp model:Brit Hi Gain. Drive: 5. Bass:1. Mid:2. Treble:7. Reverb:off.
Effect - compressor: 5
Additional overdubs came from the Tom Anderson into the POD and TriAxis using
various chorus and tremolo effects from the TC *G-Force* effects unit.

someday

The lead part was played on the Tom Anderson and then tracked using a 1978 Strat
fitted with EMG pickups. Both guitars were played through the TriAxis
(Lead 1 green mode).
Additional weight was added to the track using the Les Paul and POD with a
moderate drive setting.

so young

The acoustic rhythm tracks were recorded using the Taylor and a 12-string Martin,
both miked with an AKG C414.
The lead part was played on the EMG Strat into the POD with the following settings:
Amp model:Small Tweed. Drive:6. Bass:3. Mid:2. Treble:6. Reverb:off.
Effect - compressor:5.
Further overdubs were played on the Les Paul through the POD using similar
settings.

toss the feathers

Again the main guitar part was doubled using the EMG Strat through the TriAxis
(Lead 2 green mode) and then through the POD with a Brit. Hi Gain setting. A third
track using the Les Paul and POD added even more weight to the middle section!

what can i do

A Gibson ES345 with the tone rolled off via its tone selector was used along with an
extreme amount of compression from the TC *G-Force* and a Focusrite *Red 3*!
The 'Small Tweed' setting on the POD provided the amp sound (with no drive).

guitar tablature explained

Guitar music can be notated three different ways: on a musical stave, in tablature, and in rhythm slashes

RHYTHM SLASHES are written above the stave. Strum chords in the rhythm indicated. Round noteheads indicate single notes.

THE MUSICAL STAVE shows pitches and rhythms and is divided by lines into bars. Pitches are named after the first seven letters of the alphabet.

TABLATURE graphically represents the guitar fingerboard. Each horizontal line represents a string, and each number represents a fret.

4th string, 2nd fret   1st & 2nd strings open, played together   open D chord

definitions for special guitar notation

SEMI-TONE BEND: Strike the note and bend up a semi-tone (1/2 step).

WHOLE-TONE BEND: Strike the note and bend up a whole-tone (whole step).

GRACE NOTE BEND: Strike the note and bend as indicated. Play the first note as quickly as possible.

QUARTER-TONE BEND: Strike the note and bend up a 1/4 step.

BEND & RELEASE: Strike the note and bend up as indicated, then release back to the original note.

COMPOUND BEND & RELEASE: Strike the note and bend up and down in the rhythm indicated.

PRE-BEND: Bend the note as indicated, then strike it.

PRE-BEND & RELEASE: Bend the note as indicated. Strike it and release the note back to the original pitch.

UNISON BEND: Strike the two notes simultaneously and bend the lower note up to the pitch of the higher.

BEND & RESTRIKE: Strike the note and bend as indicated then restrike the string where the symbol occurs.

BEND, HOLD AND RELEASE: Same as bend and release but hold the bend for the duration of the tie.

BEND AND TAP: Bend the note as indicated and tap the higher fret while still holding the bend.

VIBRATO: The string is vibrated by rapidly bending and releasing the note with the fretting hand.

HAMMER-ON: Strike the first (lower) note with one finger, then sound the higher note (on the same string) with another finger by fretting it without picking.

PULL-OFF: Place both fingers on the notes to be sounded, Strike the first note and without picking, pull the finger off to sound the second (lower) note.

LEGATO SLIDE (GLISS): Strike the first note and then slide the same fret-hand finger up or down to the second note. The second note is not struck.

NOTE: The speed of any bend is indicated by the music notation and tempo.

SHIFT SLIDE (GLISS & RESTRIKE): Same as legato slide, except the second note is struck.

TRILL: Very rapidly alternate between the notes indicated by continuously hammering on and pulling off.

TAPPING: Hammer ("tap") the fret indicated with the pick-hand index or middle finger and pull off to the note fretted by the fret hand.

PICK SCRAPE: The edge of the pick is rubbed down (or up) the string, producing a scratchy sound.

MUFFLED STRINGS: A percussive sound is produced by laying the fret hand across the string(s) without depressing, and striking them with the pick hand.

NATURAL HARMONIC: Strike the note while the fret-hand lightly touches the string directly over the fret indicated.

PINCH HARMONIC: The note is fretted normally and a harmonic is produced by adding the edge of the thumb or the tip of the index finger of the pick hand to the normal pick attack.

HARP HARMONIC: The note is fretted normally and a harmonic is produced by gently resting the pick hand's index finger directly above the indicated fret (in parentheses) while the pick hand's thumb or pick assists by plucking the appropriate string.

PALM MUTING: The note is partially muted by the pick hand lightly touching the string(s) just before the bridge.

RAKE: Drag the pick across the strings indicated with a single motion.

TREMOLO PICKING: The note is picked as rapidly and continuously as possible.

ARPEGGIATE: Play the notes of the chord indicated by quickly rolling them from bottom to top.

SWEEP PICKING: Rhythmic downstroke and/or upstroke motion across the strings.

VIBRATO DIVE BAR AND RETURN: The pitch of the note or chord is dropped a specific number of steps (in rhythm) then returned to the original pitch.

VIBRATO BAR SCOOP: Depress the bar just before striking the note, then quickly release the bar.

VIBRATO BAR DIP: Strike the note and then immediately drop a specific number of steps, then release back to the original pitch.

additional musical definitions

	(accent)	• Accentuate note (play it louder).
	(accent)	• Accentuate note with great intensity.
	(staccato)	• Shorten time value of note.
⊓		• Downstroke
V		• Upstroke

D.%. al Coda

D.C. al Fine

tacet

• Go back to the sign (%), then play until the bar marked *To Coda* ⊕ then skip to the section marked ⊕ *Coda*.

• Go back to the beginning of the song and play until the bar marked *Fine* (end).

• Instrument is silent (drops out).

• Repeat bars between signs.

• When a repeated section has different endings, play the first ending only the first time and the second ending only the second time.

NOTE: Tablature numbers in parentheses mean: 1. The note is sustained, but a new articulation (such as hammer on or slide) begins.
2. A note may be fretted but not necessarily played.

erin shore (intro)

Traditional, arranged by Andrea Corr, Caroline Corr, Sharon Corr & Jim Corr

forgiven, not forgotten

Words & Music by Andrea Corr, Caroline Corr, Sharon Corr & Jim Corr

only when i sleep

Words & Music by Andrea Corr, Caroline Corr, Sharon Corr Jim Corr, John Shanks, Paul Peterson & Oliver Leiber

But it's on-ly when I sleep,___ see you in my dreams, got me spin-ning

round and round,___ turn-ing up-side down.___ I hear you breathe
But I on-ly hear you breathe

sleep, got me spin-ning round and round,___ turn-ing up-side down.___
But it's on-ly when I

someday

Words & Music by Andrea Corr, Caroline Corr, Sharon Corr, Jim Corr & David Foster

1. Frag - ments of____ our love,____
2. A frag - rant mem - or - y is

that's all____ we have,____ what we had____ was fan - ta - sy____ dreams____
soon to fade, we lived a love____ of make - be - lieve,____ dreams____

so young

Words & Music by Andrea Corr, Caroline Corr, Sharon Corr & Jim Corr

toss the feathers

Traditional, arranged by Andrea Corr, Caroline Corr, Sharon Corr & Jim Corr

what can i do

Words & Music by Andrea Corr, Caroline Corr, Sharon Corr & Jim Corr

1. I have-n't slept at all in days,
2. There's on - ly so much I can take,
3.(%) May - be there's no - thing more to say,

Chorus

No more wait - ing, no more ach - ing.

No more fight - ing, no more try - ing.

D. %. al Coda ⊕

⊕ Coda   **Chorus**

(What can I do to make you care?)

What can I do___ to make___ you love___

___ me.
(What can I do to make you love me?)

What can I do___ to make___ you care?___

Présentation De La Tablature De Guitare

Il existe trois façons différentes de noter la musique pour guitare : à l'aide d'une portée musicale, de tablatures ou de barres rythmiques.

Les **BARRES RYTHMIQUES** sont indiquées au-dessus de la portée. Jouez les accords dans le rythme indiqué. Les notes rondes indiquent des notes réciles.

La **PORTÉE MUSICALE** indique les notes et rythmes et est divisée en mesures. Cette division est représentée par des lignes. Les notes sont : do, ré, mi, fa, sol, la, si.

La **PORTÉE EN TABLATURE** est une représentation graphique des touches de guitare. Chaque ligne horizontale correspond à une corde et chaque chiffre correspond à une case.

4ème corde, 2ème case   1ère et 2ème cordes à vide, jouées simultanément   accord de ré ouvert

Notation Spéciale De Guitare : Définitions

TIRÉ DEMI-TON : Jouez la note et tirez la corde afin d'élever la note d'un demi-ton (étape à moitié).

TIRÉ PLEIN : Jouez la note et tirez la corde afin d'élever la note d'un ton entier (étape entière).

TIRÉ D'AGRÉMENT : Jouez la note et tirez la corde comme indiqué. Jouez la première note aussi vite que possible.

TIRÉ QUART DE TON : Jouez la note et tirez la corde afin d'élever la note d'un quart de ton.

TIRÉ ET LÂCHÉ : Jouez la note et tirez la corde comme indiqué, puis relâchez, afin d'obtenir de nouveau la note de départ.

TIRÉ ET REJOUÉ : Jouez la note et tirez la corde comme indiqué puis rejouez la corde où le symbole apparaît.

PRÉ-TIRÉ : Tirez la corde comme indiqué puis jouez cette note.

PRÉ-TIRÉ ET LÂCHÉ : Tirez la corde comme indiqué. Jouez la note puis relâchez la corde afin d'obtenir le ton de départ.

HAMMER-ON: Jouez la première note (plus basse) avec un doigt puis jouez la note plus haute sur la même corde avec un autre doigt, sur le manche mais sans vous servir du médiator.

PULL-OFF: Positionnez deux doigts sur les notes à jouer. Jouez la première note et sans vous servir du médiator, dégagez un doigt pour obtenir la deuxième note, plus basse.

GLISSANDO : Jouez la première note puis faites glisser le doigt le long du manche pour obtenir la seconde note qui, elle, n'est pas jouée.

GLISSANDO ET REJOUÉ : Identique au glissando à ceci près que la seconde note est jouée.

HARMONIQUES NATURELLES : Jouez la note tandis qu'un doigt effleure la corde sur le manche correspondant à la case indiquée.

PICK SCRAPE (SCRATCH) : On fait glisser le médiator le long de la corde, ce qui produit un son éraillé.

ÉTOUFFÉ DE LA PAUME : La note est partiellement étouffée par la main (celle qui se sert du médiator). Elle effleure la (les) corde(s) juste au-dessus du chevalet.

CORDES ÉTOUFFÉES : Un effet de percussion produit en posant à plat la main sur le manche sans relâcher, puis en jouant les cordes avec le médiator.

NOTE: La vitesse des tirés est indiquée par la notation musicale et le tempo.

Erläuterung zur Tabulaturschreibweise

Es gibt drei Möglichkeiten, Gitarrenmusik zu notieren: im klassichen Notensystem, in Tabulaturform oder als rhythmische Akzente.

RHYTHMISCHE AKZENTE werden über dem Notensystem notiert. Geschlagene Akkorde werden rhythmisch dargestellt. Ausgeschriebene Noten stellen Einzeltöne dar.

Im **NOTENSYSTEM** werden Tonhöhe und rhythmischer Verlauf festgelegt; es ist durch Taktstriche in Takte unterteilt. Die Töne werden nach den ersten acht Buchstaben des Alphabets benannt.
Beachte: "B" in der anglo-amerkanischen Schreibweise entspricht dem deutschen "H"!

DIE TABULATUR ist die optische Darstellung des Gitarrengriffbrettes. Jeder horizontalen Linie ist eine bestimmte Saite zugeordnet, jede Zahl bezeichnet einen Bund.

4. Saite, 2. Bund   1. & 2. Saite offen, gleichzeitig anschlagen   offener D Akkord

Erklärungen zur speziellen Gitarennotation

HALBTON-ZIEHER: Spiele die Note und ziehe dann um einen Halbton höher (Halbtonschritt).

GANZTON-ZIEHER: Spiele die Note und ziehe dann einen Ganzton höher (Ganztonschritt).

ZIEHER MIT VORSCHLAG: Spiele die Note und ziehe wie notiert. Spiele die erste Note so schnell wie möglich.

VIERTELTON-ZIEHER: Spiele die Note und ziehe dann einen Viertelton höher (Vierteltonschritt).

ZIEHEN UND ZURÜCKGLEITEN: Spiele die Note und ziehe wie notiert; lasse den Finger dann in die Ausgangposition zurückgleiten. Dabei wird nur die erste Note angeschlagen.

ZIEHEN UND NOCHMALIGES ANSCHLAGEN: Spiele die Note und ziehe wie notiert, schlage die Saite neu an, wenn das Symbol "▶" erscheint und lasse den Finger dann zurückgleiten.

ZIEHER VOR DEM ANSCHLAGEN: Ziehe zuerst die Note wie notiert; schlage die Note dann an.

ZIEHER VOR DEM ANSCHLAGEN MIT ZURÜCKGLEITEN: Ziehe die Note wie notiert; schlage die Note dann an und lasse den Finger auf die Ausgangslage zurückgleiten.

AUFSCHLAGTECHNIK: Schlage die erste (tiefere) Note an; die höhere Note (auf der selben Saite) erklingt durch kräftiges Aufschlagen mit einem anderen Finger der Griffhand.

ABZIEHTECHNIK: Setze beide Finger auf die zu spielenden Noten und schlage die erste Note an. Ziehe dann (der nochmals anzuschlagen) den oberen Finger der Griffhand seitlich - abwärts ab, um die zweite (tiefere) Note zum klingen zu bringen.

GLISSANDOTECHNIK: Schlage die erste Note an und rutsche dann mit dem selben Finger der Griffhand aufwärts oder abwärts zur zweiten Note. Die zweite Note wird nicht angeschlagen.

GLISSANDOTECHNIK MIT NACHFOLGENDEM ANSCHLAG: Gleiche Technik wie das gebundene Glissando, jedoch wird die zweite Note angeschlagen.

NATÜRLICHES FLAGEOLETT: Berühre die Saite über dem angegebenen Bund leicht mit einem Finger der Griffhand. Schlage die Saite an und lasse sie frei schwingen.

PICK SCRAPE: Fahre mit dem Plektrum nach unten über die Saiten - klappt am besten bei umsponnenen Saiten.

DÄMPFEN MIT DER SCHLAGHAND: Lege die Schlaghand oberhalb der Brücke leicht auf die Saite(n).

DÄMPFEN MIT DER GRIFFHAND: Du erreichst einen percussiven Sound, indem du die Griffhand leicht über die Saiten legst (ohne diese herunterzudrücken) und dann mit der Schlaghand anschlägst.

AMMERKUNG: Das Tempo der Zieher und Glissandos ist abhängig von der rhythmischen Notation und dem Grundtempo.

Spiegazioni Di Tablatura Per Chitarra

La musica per chitarra può essere annotata in tre diversi modi: sul pentagramma, in tablatura e in taglio ritmico

IL TAGLIO RITMICO è scritto sopra il pentagramma. Percuotere le corde al ritmo indicato. Le teste arrotondate delle note indicano note singole.

IL PENTAGRAMMA MUSICALE mostra toni e ritmo ed è divisa da linee in settori. I toni sono indicati con le prime sette lettere dell'alfabeto.

LA TABLATURA rappresenta graficamente la tastiera della chitarra. Ogni linea orizzontale rappresenta una corda, ed ogni corda rappresenta un tasto.

4° corda, 2° tasto   1° e 2° corda aperte, suonate insieme   accordo D aperto

Definizioni Per Annotazioni Speciali Per Chitarra

SEMI-TONO CURVATO: percuotere la nota e curvare di un semitono (1/2 passo).

TONO CURVATO: Percuotere la nota e curvare di un tono (passo intero).

NOTA BREVE, CURVATA: percuotere la nota e curvare come indicato. Suonare la prima nota il più velocemente possibile.

QUARTO DI TONO, CURVATO: Percuotere la nota e curvare di un quarto di passo.

CURVA E LASCIA: Percuotere la nota e curvare come indicato, quindi rilasciare indietro alla nota originale.

CURVA E RIPERCUOTI: Percuotere la nota e curvare come indicato poi ripercuotere la corda nel punto del simbolo.

PRE-CURVA: Curvare la nota come indicato e quindi percuoterla.

PRE-CURVA E RILASCIO: Curvare la nota come indicato. Colpire e rilasciare la nota indietro alla tonalità indicata.

MARTELLO-COLPISCI: Colpire la prima nota (in basso) con un dito; quindi suona la nota più alta (sulla stessa corda) con un altro dito, toccandola senza pizzicare.

TOGLIERE: Posizionare entrambe le dita sulla nota da suonare. Colpire la prima nota e, senza pizzicare, togliere le dita per suonare la seconda nota (più in basso).

LEGATO SCIVOLATO (GLISSATO): Colpire la prima nota e quindi far scivolare lo stesso dito della mano della tastiera su o giù alla seconda nota. La seconda nota non viene colpita.

CAMBIO SCIVOLATO (GLISSARE E RICOLPIRE): Uguale al legato - scivolato eccetto che viene colpita la seconda nota.

ARMONICA NATURALE: Colpire la nota mentre la mano della tastiera tocca leggermente la corda direttamente sopra il tasto indicato.

PIZZICA E GRAFFIA: Il limite del pizzicato è tirato su (o giù) lungo la corda, producendo un suono graffiante.

SORDINA CON IL PALMO: La nota è parzialmente attenuato dalla mano del pizzicato toccando la corda (le corde) appena prima del ponte.

CORDE SMORZATE: Un suono di percussione viene prodotto appoggiando la mano della tastiera attraverso la corda (le corde) senza premere, e colpendole con la mano del pizzicato.

NOTA: La velocità di ogni curvatura è indicata dalle annotazioni musicali e dal tempo.